The Four Journeys

A Collection of Poetry from the works of
Shaykh Fadhalla Haeri
along the Four Journeys of Mulla Sadra

'Not until You truly see
You can never be.
You will truly see
When you know
You are the seen.'

Zahra Publications

First published in 2014

Distributed and republished in 2021

Publisher Zahra Publications

www.sfhfoundation.com

www.zahrapublications.pub

Designed and typeset in South Africa by Mizpah Marketing Concepts

Cover design by Mizpah Marketing Concepts

ISBN: 978-1-919826-81-3

Acknowledgments

Thank you to Moriam Grillo, Ayesha Powell, Muna Bilgrami, Muneera Haeri, Ahmed Baasith Sheriff, Anjum Jaleel, Abbas Bilgrami, Leyya Kalla and others for their assistance on this production.

Contents

Publisher's Note

Zahra Publications would like to thank Shaykh Fadhlalla Haeri for his active participation and support in the production of the Four Journeys anthology of poetry. The photographs in each chapter were personally taken by Shaykh Fadhlalla Haeri during a period of four years when he was travelling on his boat around the Indian Ocean and the East African coast. They were selected by the author to reflect the appropriate stages along the respective journeys. The paper and cover were also personally selected by the author. Only 300 copies of this anthology have been printed, each uniquely numbered and signed by the author, rendering this collection a rare collector's item amongst seekers and poetry enthusiasts.

Foreword

Poetry is truly the language of the soul. It speaks with an immediacy that is suited to conveying sudden realizations and nuanced states of consciousness.

In these poems Shaykh Fadhlalla reveals to us his own interior reality, the space in which he abides. He is a man who thinks in English, writes in Arabic, and might be found singing in Persian among the ruins of ancient Nishapur. In these playful glorifications we find our own minds and hearts flashing between seen and unseen, immanence and transcendence, earth and heaven.

Let us follow Shaykh Fadhlalla into the unseen, let us disappear with him into the ecstasy of oneness, let us return from that oneness hand in hand, friend with friend, soul with soul, grateful for the appearance of this manyness, every detail of which reminds us continually we are one, we are one, we are one.

Each poem is a template of an aspect of the invisible world, a signature of the unseen. Each poem is a telescope sighting through the vast distances and at the same time the mirror reflecting our own consciousness. And let us be thankful that in this world there are souls like his that burn bright and illuminate this earth, this body, this heart.

~Shaykh Kabir Helminski

Introduction

O human you are struggling towards your Lord and striving until you come to know Him. Quran 84:6

The notion of the complete human being or the '*Insan al-kamil*' was addressed by early Islamic scholars and masters following the model of the Prophet and his exemplary conduct. Prophets, sages, imams and sufi masters have elaborated upon a life fulfilled by enlightenment and God-realisation. This experience is the outcome of leaving behind self-illusion, identity and duality.

Quality life begins when your direction is clear and you accept responsibility and accountability for your actions. Human needs and desires are endless. Acceptance of this fact is the first step. This is followed by a living faith and trust in God's perfect mercy and justice, irrespective of circumstance. Then comes the security, knowledge and experience of divine guidance through one's own soul and purified heart – a desirable destiny.

All prophets and messengers have travelled by trust and witnessed the light of Allah at all times. They lived with inner certainty and contentment. The illumined being also experiences the presence of Allah's mercy and grace; such beings can only be in ecstatic gratitude at heart, even when responding to earthly challenges. This is the complete person. Those people who have reached that station are the appropriate guides and role models to be followed.

Numerous enlightened masters in the past have guided and helped humanity toward higher consciousness and happiness. Mulla Sadra (d.1640 CE) described the journey of the seeker's ascent into higher consciousness in four stages. In this work I have adopted and modified his four journeys to frame the poetry appropriately.

The First Journey is from the creation towards Truth. The Second is by Truth in Truth. The Third Journey directly mirrors the First as it is from Truth to creation. The Fourth Journey is by Truth amongst creation.

Many people have had some experience of the First Journey – especially when they want to escape affliction and discord. Epiphanies and special insights hint at the Second Journey. Helping and serving others with empathy and generosity reflects the Third Journey. The Fourth Journey is a rare undertaking where outer effort and sacrifice is balanced by inner reliance upon the origin of life – Allah. One hand gropes in darkness, while the other hangs on light.

It is inevitable that at times the sincere seeker will experience states which reflect different aspects of the journey. However, a state (*hal*) or a momentary spiritual illumination (*ishraq*) is different from a station (*maqam*), the latter being when one is firmly established within this condition and remains steadfast on the Path.

The need for a teacher, guide or mentor is essential throughout the journeys, especially the Second Journey. The borders between these stations are not rigid; they overlap and are hazy in the flow of time and sequence. An aspect of the Fourth Journey, for example, can be realised whilst on the First.

As for those intoxicated with His love, they start by witnessing Allah's essence in bewilderment, and then descend to attributes and existential realities. The wayfarer on the other hand, is constantly concerned with Allah's manifestation and His relationship with creations, meanings and attributes, ending with witnessing the Essence. The God-intoxicated ones descend from Him towards creation whilst the normal wayfarer ascends from creation towards the Creator.

This compilation is a poetic rendering of the human paradox and our journey in life toward God-consciousness and the supreme Reality. Our inner spirit leads us passionately and relentlessly toward that perfect destiny. Indeed we are bracketed between our outer humanity and inner divinity. The driving forces in life are to connect (the end of separation) and to continue (timelessness).

I. The First Journey

I will exhaust him as he ascends. Quran 74:17

The traveller realises with maturity and spiritual insight all the previous illusions and falsehood which were necessary for the animal self to evolve and act as a buffer for the effulgent soul and its sacred light. This journey begins with ignorance and ends by piercing the cocoon of darkness. It exemplifies the declaration that there is none other than the One and leads to fleeing from conflicting creations to the one Creator. Multiplicity is confusion and unity is blissful fusion.

The First Journey ends by discarding the veils of identity, separation and conditioned consciousness which limit us within space and time. Most intelligent human beings are propelled by the innate forces of seeking universal connectedness and timelessness, thereby enduring the illusion of the cycles of beginnings and ends.

The First Journey consists of traversing the material regions, the spiritual realms, and arriving at the Essence. Most of the difficulties and pain which the seeker encounters occur within the First Journey. Stripping of specific identities ego profiles and values are essential pre-conditions to realising the truth of Reality.

Most of the poems in this section reflect the state of a serious quest propelled by avoidance of what is false and temporary whilst looking for the state that is constant, reliable and free from the constraints of existence. It is movement from diversity to unity and from dispersion to gatheredness. At the beginning of creation there was only the One and in truth there has only been the One. The traveller is striving toward that sacred Reality.

I. The First Journey

With disappointment
fear,
anger and strife
there is some hope
for a better life;
if not soon
it may be in the afterlife.
We wish to leave behind
whatever caused harm
looking forward to
liberation,
peace and joy.
This is the hopeful path
from creation to Creator,
but be warned
for near the end
there is no way
to return.

2. The Passage of Time

The day flashes by
in and out,
dances about,
to the instant tune of Time.
Silhouetted on the screen of illusion,
slipping down the sand dune of existence,
perched on the edge of a vast desert
the infinite non-existence.
But for he who seeks the Truth
Time is long and tedious,
for where is its beginning
and where is its end?
For the common man
Time is to be conquered,
to be killed.
Killing the stranger,
killing the nomadic tribe,
wandering here and there,
sometimes staying long
sometimes short - all relative!
Challenging the fixed city
with its structures and rules,
its sand and earth are veiled by asphalt.
But how to stop the shifting sand
covering the globe,
the movement of the hour glass
or the darting electron?
So fast yet still.

3. Step with Caution

Don't step on the ants
for you may kill one,
and if you kill one
you kill all.

When you cut a tree
you are on trial.
Your intention is evidence,
and if you are condemned, then
the cloud will tell the rains
to roll fast down the hill
and wash out earthly crimes,
and rush down to Mother Ocean
with the news of punishment.
Then the birds will disappear,
the sky will thunder
and the countryside be set alight:
to rejuvenate,
to remind,
to mend,
to pour out love,
interspersed with thunderclaps
and lightning to ignite,
to prepare for the birds of paradise,
to perch and drink
on the evergreen tree free of blight.
And the ants will re-build again
In praise of life and light.

4. Sleepwalking

"I am normal," the voice declared.
"Leave me to sleep
for this is my real condition.
Do not discuss or fuss,
condemning my wide open eyes,
your label of 'wakefulness'
falls on a frozen courtyard.

My open eyes simply remind me
of yesterday
and tomorrow,
forgetting now.
lost between the veils
of past and future,
lost in dreams."

"So please do not discuss or fuss—
the blind misleading the blind,
dreaming within a dream
with no dawn or dusk.
That too, I am told,
is the real condition
of those in addiction.
Then I hear there are others
considered awakened,
not in stupor or sleep.
I am told there are others
besides us common sleep-walkers,
but I am not amongst them."

5. *Morning in the Plantation*

Parchment-like, thin as a muslin veil,
The radiant green banana fronds
glistened and waved farewell
to the morning mist.
Like victory flags
parading on the hilltop,
blending the orchard songs
of buds, trees and palm fronds,
merging with colours, forms and stillness
unified in the early light
in delight, in symphony, in harmony
cloaked in white,
from light unto light
all defined by changing shadows
confined to hills and meadows
without which there can be no vision
nor desperation for divine admission.
And awakening into colourless stillness
into the presence of Light-beyond-light
the boundless Essence
behind and in front
and within all sights—
Allah-Hu.

6. To Give Up

Hold my hand tight.
Please hold me
to stop my confusion
and constant illusion
of changing realities
with no certainty.
Shapes dissolving
into shades,
facts into fiction.
Was it the cause
or is it the effect?

Hug me tight.
Losing awareness of otherness
there remains no defect,
no assumption,
expectation
or judgement
and no new point of view.
For truly there is no point
other than the original sacred point.

7. Journey of the Wayfarer

The first step on the Path
begins with sincere and
committed connection
with a sympathetic teacher,
who parts with information
which sparks transmission
enabling the seeker to yield to submission
and unburden through heartfelt confession,
a cleansing that leads to Divine Permission
enabling the seeker to take
positive corrective action
leading to transformation—
a full life without omission.

8. Original Love

The gale has blown away my past,
the thick haze of the summer day
has taken away all sense of direction.
Moment is timeless at last.
Whilst Original Love is the addiction,
even when the breeze of mercy
cools the heart in my volcanic breast,
the inner ashes burn bright
and the heart illumines shadows,
for it is possessed,
obsessed
by the Original Love
in Its timeless zone
of bewildering passion
that is forever,
beyond all time or place,
then, now and before the past.

9. Helping

You have come to help,
demonstrating separation
veiling oneness,
expanding reason,
rationalized illusions.
Little comfort now
agony forever!

Help is real only
when all needs cease,
desires erased,
thoughts no more,
distance vanished,
visions banished.

Then your help is sacred
helping what never needs
mention or attention.
Even now, was and ever is,
that is sacred help.

10. Weeping Noah

Noah[1] always cried:
Was it loneliness?
Was it fear or anger?
Was it for people or from people?

Noah kept on crying,
day and night—
the Book says centuries.
Soon he was ignored
by those near and far
a familiar sound—ignored.

When he died,
the earth and heaven cried,
human memory postponed.
Truth can never be banished.
Now all of us weep.

1 'Noah' is derived from the verb 'to weep'

II. Changing Hearts

The self misleads
and the pure heart leads.
The direction is clear,
Mother Essence is awaiting,
effulgent with eternal Presence.

The sick heart aches
for its light to lead
and for the journey to succeed.
Returning to the sacred nest
in absolute Presence
where nothing was ever absent,
the heart brought about the change
to where perfection has ever-remained.

12. The Habit

Gives life and
takes it away—
worn tightly,
worn out
but inseparable.
In tatters
without falling off.
A humbling reminder
of dependency connections,
two reflections,
the habit lives on.
The inhabitants
come and go,
flickering stars
near and far,
often unnoticed
in another life:
"Where was I?"
"Who was I?"

In another life
I became a mirror
to reflect life.
Not fully alive,
just reflecting life
with the shadow
of death hanging around.

13. Troubled Soul

The soul is never troubled.
It is you who carries its shadow,
reflecting alienation and exile.
It is you,
your soul's light lies within you,
it is your self that seeks freedom.

It is you
who are desperate to connect and continue.
It is you,
drawn to the soul
to end the illusion
and realize
the brilliant conclusion.

It is you,
ever in trouble,
until you give in
and live as a soul.
Liberated.
In bliss.

14. Danger

Unstoppable,
the drive to the edge
risking all
the quest for boundlessness.
A new birth not biology,
primal nature,
not personal or conditioned,
beyond limits of judgment,
between the visible and the invisible,
in the original Oneness.
No mental activities there,
no human uncertainty there,
no idea of why and where,
beyond the idea of security or danger
all is in the One here or there,
when your life's work is done,
by the One,
unto the One.

15. Living Heart

In bewilderment,
confusing separation,
catching a raindrop
as it settles.
Vibrating stillness
to heal,
give in,
reassured by
the light within.
A surrendered self
ruled by soul,
supreme Presence,
effulgent heart
dancing in joy,
the greatest
sacred play,
ecstatic beingness.

16. From Dunya to Light

Shifting realities
betraying its lovers,
confusing mists,
dark sights with rare insights.

Seeking grace,
tracing the sacred
through sparks of passion
for a way out.

Darkness,
fear,
grief,
praying for relief.

Beyond confinements of
Dunya's[2] veils
where there is only Light,
Light upon Light!

2 'Dunya' refers to a basic and earthly state.

17. Realisation

To deny
the battles of separation,
darkened connection:
praying for a fusion
to be consumed in Oneness
the ultimate conclusion,
first and last in union,
the hidden ever-apparent,
utter perfection,
Absolute Oneness
within itself,
before itself,
after itself,
only one self,
Cosmic Spirit.

18. Anticipation

Before the passion of love
he thought he is 'dead'?
Departing helplessly,
missing the present
in transition,
awaiting resolution,
praying for good outcomes:
life blessed by love
ever-cherished,
not subject to birth or death,
ever-present,
beyond anticipation.

19. Self and Soul

Bewildered:
"Who am I?"
"Where am I?"
"Why?"
"Where next?"
"How?"
The self ever wonders,
exhausted and desperate.
the soul knows it all,
the original, singular all,
before flow or lights glow,
before high or low,
here or there,
now or later.
Present in all,
the soul knows it all.

20. Perfect Destiny

A hesitant voice asks:
"Can't we die together?"
The inner voice whispers,
"Unity and life is forever.
When separation vanishes,
you and I are but one.
End of illusions,
blissful conclusions,
perfection of Oneness."

II. The Second Journey

And with your Lord is the final abode. Quran 53:42

There are generally three stages in the Second Journey. The first involves the loss of identity and selfhood. Much bewilderment and confusion accompanies this stage. The second stage is the experience of higher attributes and qualities associated with truth. Here one realises the extent of hypocrisy, denial and assumptions that we are caught in. The third stage is that of annihilation into the Essence and attributes. The mysterious divine power takes over totally until consciousness vanishes into sacred oblivion – utter Oneness. This is being enfolded within the 'inner *ka'bah*' where there is no-thingness except the original singularity. The attributes of Allah, His names and traits are realised by their truth, whilst the sense of I-ness is totally obliterated. The unity of Allah's names, attributes and realities are now effulgent.

Now the sublime, perfect beauty and majesty of Oneness within the universe is evident. The inseparability of duality from singularity becomes the natural lens by which existence is seen. A butterfly has emerged from the caterpillar. A new creation has emerged, as described by the Qur'an as different or new.

Many human beings have glimpsed this station during spiritual practices. Labels such as 'epiphany', 'sudden insights' or 'cracks in consciousness' are given. These hint at the loss of identity, selfhood and time. The past life is a hazy memory; space and time are thin veils upon the effulgent presence.

Most of the poems in this section express the feeling of sacred presence and the end of absence. Truth is the only self-sustaining Reality. *La ilaha illa'llah* is declared and all else are passing shadows.

I. The Second Journey

There is a barrier
between your old self
and the newly discovered soul.
Like a bad dream
giving way to a beautiful day.

The second station
is the zone of the Absolute.
There is only Oneness.
No you
or anything else —
the Infinite Eternal,
the Real beyond description.
This is the no-thingness
from where
cosmos is born —
beginnings and ends
are one.

2. Come Back

Now just come!
Plunge into light,
melt in love,
diffused in its ocean
die into the moment,
to live forever
in your birthplace
without form,
before existence.
Come without care,
discard all your burdens,
be free,
bare.
Bury your heart and face
in a timeless embrace.
There remains one face,
reflecting Beauty,
utter Majesty,
eternal Reality.

3. Tourism and Travel

The tourist prepares
backpack, suitcase or bundle
to take along,
but when the time comes
for the real journey
you leave possessions behind.
Plunging into the unknown
the journey begins
to the intended destiny.

To experience a new life,
boundless vistas
beyond mind and limbs,
utter harmony and peace,
where past desires and needs
are erased
in the courtyard of contentment
beyond discernments,
thoughts and existence,
journey's perfect end.

4. Fate

Fate is Now.
It is the experience of the moment,
not the past or future.
It is the Presence,
the sacred sun,
which wipes out shadows of doubt
filling the cup of life.

The wind of Destiny
blows one over the sand dune.
In the hourglass,
trembling as life,
whispering to the soul
the true Presence
on its journey.
Leaving behind
traces of the past,
for the Sacred Soul
is free from past, present and future
and sings only
the melody of eternal Now.

5. Illusion of Arrival

The seeker is told
to purify and stabilize,
be conscious and maximize,
to be at source
and remain constant
in order to realize
whatever appears out there
is a reflection of what is already at heart in here.
Reflections embracing an identity,
flowing along its own destiny,
where certainty, hope and fear
exchange glances and appear
as flashes of a shy moon
and where new images and things
veil, and occasionally reveal,
a presence that blows away
all pasts and futures.
And the song of the Essence
attracts stillness,
pure beingness,
blissful gatheredness,
all engulfed by
the ecstasy within the
miracle of Oneness.

6. On the Edge

The edge— thrilling!
Any edge,
boundary,
or transition,
sea, mountain or life.
For an instant,
time leads to eternity.

7. That Is It

Enhancing identities
to write memoirs.
Inventing posterity,
helpless futility.
Afloat in a timeless ocean
with no shores,
name or a place on any map;
simply there
but never to be found.
Here, there and everywhere,
all lost within It.

8. Beam of Truth

With truth, nothing matters
as everything is embedded in truth.
Its appearance is due to it,
emanating or returning to it.
Thus the power of truth,
traced within its offspring,
into a world of challenges and confusion
where everything appears possible,
yet in truth they are all images
pretending to reflect the Real,
misguiding as substances
within places and instances,
flashes of truth here and there
giving the appearance
of Reality that belongs to nowhere,
masked by shadows,
temporary illusions
alluding to Perfect Grace
and divine conclusions.

9. Playing One

It may seem absurd:
differentiated Oneness
justified as love,
play practice.
What was before,
what comes after,
the confused middle
connected to both sides,
expands and contracts
yielding to its field,
cycles within cycles
connected to the One origin,
playing it all along
within perfect emptiness
One beingness.

10. Primal Obsession

The echo of separation,
the split,
the crack!
Whatever appears
knows its origin.
Obsessed by Unity,
propelled to end separation,
attaining final rest.
A mirror of the original,
all else—shadows
reflecting *Lahūt*[3].

3 Realm of Divinity

II. Presence

The past is dead,
the future is ahead,
the present the real thread
between heart and head,
between known and unknown,
formed and unformed.

The present is
the child of the past
and the parent
of what will be known,
now being cast and hewn.
So if my past was
full of fear and desire,
then my present is
turmoil and fire.
But if my past actions
were devoid of agitation,
anxiety, greed or frustration,
then my present will be
towards greater freedom and liberation.

The more you live
fully in the present
the closer you are
to the perfect Real,
in you latent.

So be in the Now
and remain ever young,
the child of the present,
forever now.

12. Allah's Will

Allah's purpose
is to be known
by seeing the meaning
behind what is shown,
and this can only happen
if the veil is torn.

Now, you may ask,
"Where is this veil?
What color?
How thick?
And how can I prevail?"

The question itself confirms the veil!
And rational pursuit
will be to no avail.
For the veil is naught
but your creation
and its source is
your self-identification.

To ascend
transcend your senses
to the origin of the descent,
fulfilling your destiny.

13. Actor's Shadow

You are the actor
and acted upon,
among the audience,
changing roles and costumes,
sometimes with conviction,
other times with distraction,
always hoping for applause and confirmation,
thus veiled by self-deception.

Giving purpose and meaning
to the vacant hall,
packed with confused people,
nations and cultures
caught by timeless sparks,
dancing through patterns and designs
labeled as individuals and shapes,
with feelings and make-believe,
endless illusions or conclusions.

Yet the actor's soul is a spark of Perfection
by Grace of the One Light
leading actor and audience
to the Quest of the Source
from where all emanated,
creating the illusions of separation
of audience, actors
and other shadows.

14. Reality of Illusions

Time is the lens
through which you read space
and what appears from the web
of creational veils
layer upon layer,
change after exchange,
in perpetual flux
with an illuminating core,
the constant source
invisible indivisible,
permeating time and space
announcing the Only Real
which creates all illusions
within time and space.

15. My Existence

My existence
drawn from Light
expresses glorification,
to witness
gatheredness in dispersion
and dispersal of gatheredness
in blessed bewilderment,
in nearness of distance
and distance of nearness,
ecstatic speechlessness!

Exhausting is the quest of perfection
when inwardness is covered
by layers of outwardness
and firstness by lastness
and heavens by earthiness.

His heavens encompass His earth,
His fire is from His garden—
all of it is His garden!
My soul is a beam of His Light.

His Light is beyond sight
but within time and space and beyond
His Presence is veiled by absence
the Ever-Living Delight,
Light upon Light.

16. The End is a Mirage

At first the mind is pure
you are one without counting
that purity will soon be coloured
and each mind develop its habits
experiences, changes and new views
the world's whirlwind distracts
the original mind is a distant memory
a yearning for endless beginning
where you knew nothing
and yet the light of knowledge
sufficed everything.

17. Perfect Journey

Some call it 'wholeness',
others 'holiness',
but boundless Presence
or universal Essence
has no cause or preference.

Wisdom is to plunge
with no safety harness,
disappear without self
or anticipating grace,
into oblivion and dust.
Then flashes of perfection
sing and call.

Clouds of earthly smells
covered by yesterday,
confused by to-day,
missing presence,
chasing holiness
or other illusory absence,
until death brings real life
and completes the journey of
wholesomeness.

18. Form and Meaning

Inseparable,
appearing differentiable,
no particle without energy,
no form without meaning.
Separations masking seamless connection,
convenient illusions,
delaying the calling—
conclusion.

19. Bewildered

Tests,
challenges,
surprises—all emotions.
The whole cacophony
leading to blinding flashes
where madness and sanity fuse,
where a sacred bewilderment binds!
Now where to?
How and why?
When all subsides,
you know
it is only
Now.

20. *Listen*

From silence
I hear the whisper.
"Here, here,"
It says.
"There and here,"
It says.
"Everywhere,"
It says.
"And nowhere,"
It says.
"Just listen,
only listen.
Do not respond,
for you are not even here,"
It says.
"Then you are really you,"
It says.

21. Connected- Not the Same

The path is not home.
The teacher is not knowledge.
The prophet is not God.
The beginning is not the end.
They all connect,
meeting in original Oneness.

Your heart flows with love:
you may even discern or reason
what comes and goes,
the effect is the overflow
permeating like stardust
painting its colours,
impermanent rainbows,
light connecting with water in space,
at home with its beingness.

22. At the Spot

Then it happened.
All interests ceased.
The sparks consumed the forest,
no trace left.
A story passed on —
what was inside
now worn outside.
Truth has no side,
always spot on.
But who is to spot it?
How can there be you and it?
  At the spot
there is only the spot.
Everywhere else,
with illusions of trace,
the fog of otherness,
gently introducing Oneness.

23. To Be

Sparks piercing all,
expressions that ignite
beams of light
in the darkness of blackness
tell the story of passion,
not arrival, not happiness
simply acceptance —beingness.
Unshielded truth,
unbearable
except to itself,
a cosmic cry
"Where is it?"
"Who and why?"
Your three notes
exploded my universe,
to show me the Real,
catching Its truth
returning to the origin:
One Itself.

24. Illusions and Conclusions

A complete circle
sings and sings soundly.
The end has no end
nor any beginning,
just a complete circle
traced in my heart
bursting out to declare.

Falsehood carries traces of reason.
Our soul carries
the awareness of
here and there
the perfect abode
beyond all that is,
here or there,
infinite circles of light
follow hearts that return
to their home,
the perfect abode!

25. Past, Present and Now

Sometime ago
I didn't exist.
Before that
nothing existed.
Conceived in the dark womb
a journey towards the tomb.
The present carries colours of the past
towards its future.

The hypnotic breeze
parting shadows
perceptions and deceptions,
masquerading as realities,
seeking origin – the Real!
Ascending along the arc,
threading the finite,
propelled by the infinite,
all in the present,
the sacred moment.

26. *One and Two*

From two emerges one,
miracle of the womb!
Another unfoldment returning
consciousness to eternal Being.
The One
nourishing others,
held by grace
of none other.

27. *Sparks*

Mirrored sparks,
illumined space,
reduced distance,
ending absence.
Light of Oneness,
fusion,
no shadows,
no illusions,
no confusions.
One spark
connecting all lights,
every delight
One.

III. The Third Journey

Look back again, do you find any fault.

And look back again, your sight will come to you subdued. Quran 67:3-4

Now we have removed from you your veil, so your sight now is sharp. Quran 50:22

The Third Journey is from Truth towards creation 'relying upon Truth'. This station completes the refinement of conduct. It is the station of witnessing the realms of power (*jabarut*), the spiritual realms (*malakut*), the material realm (*mulk*), and illumination by knowledges from the attributes, actions and Essence. The butterfly now experiences a new life and is often baffled and surprised with respect to the sleep-walking world – countless caterpillars.

In my own case it was several months of bewilderment before I could function normally and put up with the importance that my friends and family gave to daily normal life. The Prophetic practices are very helpful as shields from human absurdities which are labelled as normal or real.

When you have tasted the boundlessness and infinitude of singularity you find everything else is jarring and repulsive. There have been many descriptions of people who had immense difficulty functioning after their return to creation. We consider the animal self and ego as normal and the effect of the Second Journey is to render you as a soul without any encumbrance. Thus it is quite a shock to be amongst people who are oblivious to their real nature – the spiritual light within. The poems in this section reflect aspects of my state, thoughts and conditions as relating to the Third Journey.

I. The Third Journey

Since you have body and mind
your return to creation
connects the finite
to the Eternal Infinite
as a messenger of truth.
You can sing
like a free bird
even though only a few
hear and transform.
Your mind differentiates
while your heart
is the abode
of Sacred Light.

2. The Curse of the Bird

Don't shoot the bird,
for you will hurt the tree
and upset the bee
and the pregnant goat will abort,
and the reeds will protest,
and the stars will flicker
and demand justice
before the heavenly court.

But the dead bird's soul
has already recorded its song
on the tablet of human wrongs,
in the heaven beyond,
claiming its right to know
who authorized man to take
that which he cannot make?
Who does he think he is?
Drunk in stupor, he is
Powerless, except for little.
He is cursed by shame,
dethroned, in ill fame,
engulfed by his inner flame.
But who is to blame?
Surely not the bird?

3. Show Me

Show me your leader
and I know who you will be.
Show me your deed
and I know who you are.
Show me your parents
and I know what makes you think you are.
Show me your food
and I meet your animal.
Show me your nothingness
and I know your clarity of everythingness.
Be nothing!
For that is the entry
to original light,
the flight to Eternal Light.

4. The Boat of No Return

Do not suffer
or be sad
or complain,
for the boat of our journey
will not return.

I could not tell you this before –
I still cannot explain –
be patient, I shall try.

In fact the boat had left
before it arrived.
The sequence is the reverse
of what we are accustomed to,
like the deception of a mirror
your right becomes your left—
habitual adjustment.

We sail into the dusk
along the wind of destiny
towards the final beginning
with no city ahead,
whilst the dead ones on board
appease and mourn the travelling dead.
The dead mourning the dead!

But the pure hearts of light
already know their destiny.
From home to home they journey.

5. The Clouds of Mercy

I can't remember
I have even forgotten
what it is to forget
like a cloud
that cannot recall its mother ocean
nor can it foretell
where it will rain
born to be homeless
wanderer without address
short-lived but forever there
born yesterday – or was it today?
dying tomorrow – or will it be today?

But for a cloud
one day is like any day
for it only lives its moment
without an itinerary
a movement in trust
a messenger
of natural mercy
with no expectation
or reward
or fancy plans
sheer mercy,
effulgent grace.

6. Celebrations

They are endless,
as many as my weaknesses
and more.
As many as my breaths
and more.
As many as my desires and needs
and more—indeed!
My fears, hopes and happiness
all vanish in the ocean of love,
which brings forth all
and much more.
Endless is its nature
as its mysterious beginning.
To rush and catch a glimpse
of the most rare—Ever-Present—
To drive to reach the party,
ever in celebration,
to forget all
and be in pure remembrance,
everlasting celebration
and even more!

7. True Joy

Brief happiness
is an oasis of life
　　in the parched desert of change,
uncertainty of vacant souls.
But it is a fake belief
which heals the hearts of past wounds,
a moment of relief,
an echo of pre-creational joy:
Essence with no attributes,
God before creation,
Divine passion with no distraction,
the Adamic rise before infatuation,
pure joy before the so-called 'fall';
before sadness or happiness,
soul not caught by self,
free from what we term,
'life, and all.'

8. Human Journey

We like extremes
to go beyond the limits,
'breathtaking,'
like impossible loves,
'heart-breaking.'
Full moon in a desert sky,
passionate love without a why.

Beyond the furthest limits
there lies our promise
of absolute connection and timelessness,
pure beingness,
encompassing all that is visible and unseen.

A Garden of Divine Passion
where the qualification of entry
is annihilation to the world of change
and entry is through the gate
of total submission,
without qualification,
reservation,
or any condition.

9. Divine Love

You have a head.
You also have a heart.
One is the base of reason,
the other is light in every season.
When the heart is at one with reason,
then you are centered.
How can the heart's passion
be fulfilled by a passing lover?
True Love is eternal;
earthly lovers will only expose
the paradox
and prove their inability to be consumed
by their inner love
and yield to the light of true passion,
past the timeless arc
of abandonment
into the Ka'bah of the heart,
while the head is concerned
holding its zoo at bay!

As for the common folks—
they are barely touched
by the power of Divine Love,
Yet they seem to be looking for it
in every direction,
not realizing its Presence
is constant
encompassing all existence and creation.

10. Before Here Was Now

When time was not,
Was I there?
Were you there?
Who was there?

Before something and nothing
stillness gave birth to movement.

And time began
and space opened
and silence spoke
all from Jannah[4]
birth of the cosmos
everywhere and nowhere
baby earth engulfed in boundlessness
and timelessness embraced all time.
Adam's offspring
bearing the original design,
confused in space and time,
reconciling their timelessness
with birth and death.

4 Paradise

II. Binary Experience

It's all done.
In fact, gone
from where it had come.
The immovable now
ever present,
constant,
hiding behind change.

Its end before the start,
death with birth,
inseparable,
disguised as duality,
clamouring to return
to Mother Unity
where all is done
before any action,
actor, stage,
or the idea of unity.

12. It is

Don't touch,
don't look,
don't speak,
don't move,
for I will die.

Then I desire life—
a dangerous lust!
For that which is,
ever is.

13. One Face

Movements are balancers
of pressure,
to spread out,
equalize,
between rejection and acceptance,
difficulty and ease,
expansion and contraction,
the dance of balance,
two faces of One.

14. Big or Small

Big is assumed to be big
whereas it is minute.
The earth may be big for you
although it is a tiny planet
in a gigantic galaxy.
Small is assumed to be small
whereas it can be huge.
The atom is tiny in ratio
to a speck of dust,
though the space within it is vast.
So the small contains the big.
Small is small and big!
Just change the position,
come to a new proposition.

As for you,
you are small on earth.
As for your soul,
it is beyond measure!

15. Dancing

Dance without movement
music without sound
lovers who never met
drunk beyond reason
falling without wings
from above to below
or back to front.

When your soul takes you to dance
heaven's harmony swallows you up,
you are lost into your soul,
delicious ecstasy
where you know more.
The dancer dies
but the dance lives forever
honouring its origin,
the eternal soul.

16. Futile Purposefulness

Energetically
we pursue conclusions
closures or completions
ending that which began
killing what is born
images emerging from shadows
impressions of life
illusions and delusions
achievements and results
journeys anticipating arrivals
pointless points in empty space
where that which was there
had been all along, nowhere—
next door to where time was not invented,
where all conclusions are not yet born
nor purpose inaugurated
still in its universal fusion
before purposefulness
gave rise to confusion.

17. Here and There

What was there
no longer here.
What was sure
now obscure.
Ends before starts,
deaths precede births.
The alchemy of illusion,
rooted in singleness,
whose presence is veiled
to produce agonizing absence—
as presence is only known to Presence.
Yet every eye claims perception,
even sight and knowledge,
labelled as reason,
and rational conclusions,
a cover up of truth
and its unbearable glare,
agitating every stillness,
mirages of moments
somewhere, somehow,
here, there, in every place
yet not fixed in any space.

18. Take Me There

Take me to the new country
where everything is new,
always new,
constantly ever new.
Take me in a flash!
Faster than any speed I know,
beyond anything we know,
to a state where
births and deaths are not yet invented,
where sounds and sights are not yet created,
where light is not yet seen,
where twos have not yet separated,
where cosmos is still a dormant seed,
where the eternal Oneness
presides with no shadows of otherness,
where all is exclusively contained
within sacred singleness.
That country is worth belonging to!
That is the state worth longing for.
That is where love resides and overflows.
That is where time hasn't begun.
That is where all is ever new.
That is where we all belong—
ever new for those who knew!

19. Invalid

Out of balance.
Not valid.
Justice and balance
held by truth
to assume validity.
Duality left out
temporarily,
a flash of truth
for existence to realize
its invalidity,
upheld by the Ever-Valid.

20. Projects

No life without a project:
early muddles and confusions
lead to purposes and conclusions,
on to subtler horizons
where subjects and objects meet,
where beginnings and ends meet,
where shadow and light meet,
where questions and answers meet.
Then no subject or project is of concern.
Time stops.
The project unites with now—
this instant!
Constant becomes the project,
endless without beginning.
The only real project.

21. Can't You See?

Can't you see?
Please try and listen
you can only be—
just be—
not this or that!
Purely be,
then you are free,
I mean, free.

But I am afraid
You don't really see
the way to be,
for you are accustomed
and programmed to see
a bit of earth
a bit of sky
a bit of sea.
I realize now
you can't see the whole
nor can you find a way
to a new role.
So let us both give in
and let come what may
and submit to helplessness every day
and await the dawn of tomorrow
with no presumption
or any assumption,
just abandonment and submission.
That is the way of transformation.

And then together we will see
and experience firsthand
the thrill of meaning,
of how to be
not this or that,
but purely to be,
at last free,
I mean, free.

22. Decree and Destiny

Don't talk about the decree
and don't ask,
for it is about life
and life is not a subject or a task
for it has already answered the question,
so let it be.
That is the highest decree,
to be and to see.
Every event or experience
is according to its decree.
Nature is truly a perfect cosmos
and not the outcome of random chaos.
Manifestations are based on countless laws.

Some we know and see, many we don't.
The divine commands are so numerous,
to attempt to count them is superfluous.
If you made pens out of every tree
and used oceans as ink to explain
you would give up the attempt in vain!
Infinite are the possibilities in His domain,
so give up!
And sublimate,
witness and return,
then just be.

Your ultimate desired destiny
is already rooted in your heart:
intentions and actions—
if bliss is what you want, then be your soul.
and all will suffice.

23. Crime and Punishment

For every action
there is a reaction.
It may be small.
It may be big.

Once something occurs
it will have an effect,
one way or another!

What a difference
between good intentions and actions
and inappropriate ones!
Nature is not in chaos,
its order will prevail.

Good actions proceed from good intentions
where the sacred light is referenced
and dedication is evident .

Good actions multiply
and wipe out wrong ones.
What a wonderful outcome!

Another piece of good news:
responses to our wrong actions
are often postponed
in case,
reflection and repentance,
a higher displacement takes place.

Our crime is lack of connection to source
and self-punishment can only bring
replenishment for whoever is aware
seeking the presence
of light at heart.

24. Effulgent Treasure

Allah is a hidden treasure
Who loves to be known
and to that glorious station
the worthy shall surely be flown
experiencing aspects of the cosmic throne.

The journey of this ascension
born on wings of submission
fuelled by grace
of trust and realization.

You start with reason,
then go past the senses,
the good as well as nonsense!
You taste a new light from your soul,
which beckons you to move beyond your past.
This taste can then become a passion,
which ultimately burns out the old you,
yielding a new life with infinite delight.

25. Inner Sight

Wisdom starts with hindsight,
which increases our insight,
leading subsequently
to greater foresight.

But all of these states
are mere reflections of Divine Light,
visible and invisible,
energies and matter.

Illumined insights
and many more gifts
come with meanings hidden in forms,
transcending the norm.

When animal consciousness
is replaced by higher sights and lights,
then all of your past
becomes like a distant shadow
and the future promises
a state beyond description or aspiration.
In the beginning flashes of inner sight
and at the end
it is a cosmic treasure trove,
indescribable in its beauty and might.

26. Enlightened Teachers

The awakened beings
look out for true seekers
and teach,
to their inner hearts
they reach.
They do not preach.

Meanwhile they,
like everyone else,
experience constant change
and uncertainty,
whilst anchored in
inner constancy,
their contented heart at peace.
The world does not possess them,
though they may possess it,
their mistakes inconsequential,
their subtle achievements monumental,
with their followers gentle,
their love for life ample,
their lifestyle simple,
toward their Creator most humble.

So listen attentively…
if you find such a being,
make a real commitment
secure and deep,
and of enlightened wisdom
absorb and keep.
Be in this company
with no condition,
seeking permission
at the door of illumined transmission.

27. Flow of Time

Shifting sands on a windy shore,
travelling dunes
pushing upwards,
caving downwards,
gusting blows,
bending trees
followed by calm, peace and ease.

Then there are new footprints!
Hesitantly intrusive,
on the winding shore:
birds, dogs, humans and crabs,
meandering this way and that way.

The end of a day calling tomorrow,
stitching its past and future
with the endless thread of time.

Obliterating traces on sand and sea
except the passionate quest
for the True Love.
Colouring endless horizons
and shifting grains of sand
along a windy shore—
deceptively still
at its core.

28. Twinkle of an Eye

When you speak to the wind,
ride upon the rock
and travel to the stars and beyond.
Giving up all past comfort and exhaustion,
beyond helplessness and submission,
before and after
birth or death.

Only then will you have embarked
upon boundless exploration!
Only then will the oceans evaporate
and all that you have treasured
become less than a speck of dust!

After you have passed
all visions and fantasies
only then the Original Light,
with or without sound or sight,
will reveal your non-identity
in the deafening silence of harmony!
Where the spring tide of perfect will
extinguishes all other lights and shadows,
revealing the One and Only Source
of every light and apparent delight,
all in a twinkle of an eye.

29. Noah's Transit

In the ark you sit on solid timber
whilst tumbling along—
like our life
fixed and finite
yet floating away
within and beyond control,
certain in uncertainty,
secure in insecurity,
adequate in its inadequacy,
orderly in its chaos,
ever youthful and fresh
in all ages.

All of life's changes are within stillness,
travelling without moving,
within frames and forms
lies the Essence,
ever-effulgent and self-revealing.

Discharging Noah's cargo,
once anchored,
on the mount of Ararat,
in the desert of Sinai,
on the shores of the Ganges,
on the deathbed of Surrender
where there is no transit, arrival or exit,
only the boundless embrace
of the ever-Patient Beloved,
Whose Essence was and is always there.

30. Journey's End

The lonely self –
every self –
yearning for rest
in the Promised Land.
Drawing light from the soul
to console,
to assure,
to confirm
that all is secure
at the core of constant change.

Your passions drive you on
searching for the illusory treasure
along the scorching sand dunes
with no oasis in sight,
no palm groves or shades,
no stopping place,
no soul mate,
only your fragile will.
driven by an inner urge
to reconcile the twos
and millions more!
The more you look
the less you see.
The union you seek,
dispersed pearls along
the ocean floor,
in perfect randomness;
the diver, with no fear,
lands on a bed of pearls!

31. Many Days But One

As the day closes its gate,
the dusk sends its scented breeze
fragrant with blossoms and other secrets,
yielding its message:
another day erased with ease.
Day after day,
clay tablet upon clay,
racing without haste.
But what is the message of the heart?
Why did it all start?
And where will it all end?
Day after day,
night after night,
how does it move?
And to where?
From where?
How can we try to pierce
this flickering veil,
stop talking to the ghost
who is deaf and dumb, at most?
One day suffices to know
where is the arrow and whose is the bow,
who began all this
and where it will end.
The day with no night
is enough for insight,
acknowledging darkness and light
are but manifestations
of a mighty ray,
the *Nur*[5] of Allah.

5 Light

32. No Time

You were right to declare
"There is very little time."
You are right,
For in truth there is no time.

When the end and the beginning embrace
without concern for an end,
change and loss of bliss,
not in time!
Not disgraced by fear or loss.
In that house
anything can happen.
Instantly,
your love alight,
constantly,
not caught by time.

33. *Lighting a Candle*

The candle within the heart,
your soul's light,
living its presence,
when it shines
others are drawn,
claiming their share
of the sacred light.

To end a dream,
to awaken and be,
to be present
in eternal truth
universal lights
Light upon Light.

34. *Life*

Her mother has just died,
frail and unwell.
The family is relieved, except her.
The sage is asked "How can life be lost?
How can a gift be taken back?"
He whispers in her ear,
while she wipes away her tears,
"The human soul is a sacred drop
loaned from the divine ocean,
the infinite sacred Light
to which everything returns."

35. Inner and Outer

Step outside,
out – outside.
Then come back in,
come in and remain within.
Struggle and embrace all,
then again let go of all.
Now where are you?
In 'out here' or 'there'?
Far or near?
The One was always
within
land and sky,
absent from all,
present within all.

36. Present

Joyful heart,
awakened light
within you,
present,
veiled by mind,
ever-constant,
present.

37. All in a Glance

It said it all
the glance
radiated
towards the awaiting heart
tapping the original
essence of life
flashing billions of stars
upon earth
and everywhere else
the divine glance
encompasses all.

38. Hear Me

Can you hear me?
Do you read my heart?
Look into your own heart.
Hearts resonate!
They bear witness
from the One
Who always hears me.
He always hears you
too.

39. Power of Love

When love takes over
life begins.
Without giving up all
there is no answer.
Without fear or hope
there is no path.
For liberation
without needs and yearning
there will be no guidance or direction.
We are all trapped
chasing shadows,
prisoners of thought,
praying for relief,
from where there is no peace
or contentment,
missing the perfect Light,
Original Effulgence,
Oneness.

40. Life on Earth

A sample of Paradise
beautiful earth
next to lifeless darkness
children play on sand
adults muddle through
a few go to extremes
distracted transition
seeking certainty
loving eternity
perpetuity
constancy
unity
Lights of Divinity.

41. Self-Knowledge

To know yourself
stop seeing yourself
step besides yourself
beyond the self
where shadows and light merge
where the universe submerges
where Original Light emerges.

To know yourself
forget identity
face the Cosmic Reality
radiating from the Sacred Soul—
Allah.

IV. The Fourth Journey

O Prophet! Surely we have sent you as a witness, giver of good news, warner and caller to Allah by His will and luminous light. Quran 33:45-46

The Prophet taught that creation is the family of Allah and whoever is most helpful to them is most loved by Allah.

The Fourth Journey is being amongst creation whilst absorbed by truth. This is the last, most subtle, complete and perfect of the stages of the human journey. It is the end of the spiritual odyssey and connects all aspects of humanity to divinity. The master is involved with multiplicity and conflicts of creation while his heart is fully immersed within the sacred Oneness.

The four stages of the Journey reflect the meaning of the ritual of pilgrimage in Islam: the first, going towards the cave – 'Arafah; the second, being in 'Arafah with Truth, by Truth; the third, returning, testing one's conduct by sacrifice; and the fourth, returning to creation with an illumined heart.

The following prayer of Shaykh 'Abd-al Salam Ibn al-Mashish (d.1227 CE), echoes this final stage:

O Allah! Deliver me from the mires of *Tawhid*[6], and drown me in the ocean of Unity until I see nothing, hear nothing, perceive nothing, feel nothing, except through it.

The Master Al-Sabziwari taught that the First Journey is 'to Allah' from the self until one arrives at the clear horizons of the heavenly manifestations. The beginnings of the Second journey 'in Allah' is by merging with His attributes and realizing His names, then travelling to the 'loftiest horizons' and the furthermost extreme of Oneness. The Third Journey is the progression to gatheredness and universal Oneness. The Fourth Journey is differentiation after unification. The enlightened being understands otherness and deals with it whilst sustained and energised by eternal Oneness.

The poems in this section express some of my feelings and states in the Fourth Journey. The human journey is the metaphor for the descent and ascent of Adam and his offspring. We are universal souls in exile for a while on earth and our purpose is to experience descent and ascent by will, hope and prayers. The passion to know truth is a primary drive for all human beings. Good companionship, a positive outlook and constant awareness of divine presence are necessary guidelines. No one is exempt from life's challenges and afflictions. Fortunate are those who witness Allah's perfect patterns irrespective of worldly difficulties or ease.

6 Unity

I. The Fourth Journey

To serve and give unconditionally—
that is selfless.
Only soul speaks now,
generous and compassionate,
universal and passionate,
connecting hearts
yearning to be at one,
energized by souls
that know only ONE,
giving life and hope
to experience the ONE.

2. Inevitable Exit

Time has come to bid farewell
to the mulberry tree,
for time has come to embark
on the journey to meet destiny.

Back again, riding the sea,
lost in the ocean,
following the chart of devotion
with constantly changing undercurrents
uncertain about the direction
except at sunrise,
then at sunset
and in between a practice
of being diligent and acting wise
from morning to evening
from evening to dawn
leaving behind
the orchard
and the birds
and the secret whisper of
the mountain breeze
and all other comforts
that make life smooth and bring ease.

Life is indifferent
to human experience
for its only concern
is the disposal of time
in confined space
with an exit called death
to a new life beyond all change,
where the mulberry tree is ever in fruit
and Divine Love is never in dispute.

3. Season With No Reason

The seasons changed again,
summer came and went,
winter was forgotten,
autumn not even remembered,
Allah's work
already done.
No escape from the turning wheel,
nowhere to run—
one extreme leads to another,
one blind creature misleading the other,
caught in the friction
between opposites,
fighting to get back to the centre
where there is no change,
no season,
no reason,
just Is
all His.

4. One Answer

He looked at me,
through me,
and beyond horizons.
Grace is based on connection,
placing things where they belong!
Harmony and peace—
the business of life is to relate
cause and effect,
beginnings and endings,
seeking the One,
asking: "Where do I belong?"

Perfection is not confined to a place.
The mystery of your soul,
both inclusive and exclusive,
to be it,
is to stop all—
mind, tongue and limbs.

Your inner silence,
beyond space and time,
your eternal home,
the perfect abode
of no-whereness,
utter sacredness
that answers
one and all.

5. This City Has No Roads

When you are in despair
like a dolphin high on a beach,
its navigation system broken down
with no possibility of repair.
Now, give up!
Nowhere to turn,
no hope for any place or time.
Not tomorrow or next year.
Then somewhere, somehow
the instant may reveal itself
by itself,
through no effort
other than helplessness.
You come to know instantly
the meeting point of here and there,
beyond the roads
and before travel was invented.
For when thirst was created
so too was the eternal spring
in need of reaching thirsty lips,
to be acknowledged
grateful,
heartful,
hopeful.

6. Mother's Beauty

My mother was most beautiful— I had always thought.
Always there to help, give and serve,
Fulfill desires and special needs.
Her long hair was plaited—
a ladder to heaven I had often thought.
Her beauty absorbed me,
leaving only pure life in my heart,
no images or descriptions.
returning me to sacred Presence.
Pure beauty, presence and unconditional love,
all this from childhood on,
alive within me,
a living link to the Divine.

7. Being and Identity

A walking tree
is not free
it lives its past
propelled slowly to a future
carrying its memories
of fruits and roots
and the constant now
caught in stillness
and the urgency of belonging
beyond all longing
and other illusions.

8. You and I

Let me belong to You
please, let me
see You and love You.
Please take my offer,
all I have.
Make me whole
to become one
again with You
or beside You.
Take me as I am,
shattered or whole—
often either or neither.
Make me again
realize the whole,
the thrill of Oneness—
fusing You and I
as was ever,
before You and I.

9. Sacred Presence

Tell me you care,
say it again!
For it frees me
to remain as nothing,
where everything resides
before agitations began,
before lights descend and ascend,
before meanings were ascribed
to words and ideas
before care separated from neglect,
before human aspirations for what lasts,
when beginnings and ends were embracing,
ever restful in timelessness,
sharing boundless presence,
with no concern for where
when and how,
caring before any needs
or ideas of absence or presence,
being before identities,
the Real within all realities.

10. Water

Water is materialized light of light,
a spring is its emanation,
a stream is its flow in different directions,
a lake is a perfect temporary destination,
and the ocean
is the journey's ultimate rest,
the temporary completion
announcing the next cycle,
the rise and fall.

II. Fulfilled by Truth

You seek contentment and joy
convinced of this or that—
hesitant certainty.
Then for a moment your cup is full
and the blissful breeze lifts you up
whispering its tale.
Perfect, original love,
nothing beside, before or after.
The other side of mount inception
before judgment and preference,
hope or passion arrive,
declared by the vibrant smile
of a sage who has been there,
still here, embracing creation,
embraced by truth.

12. One Face

For years I faced life
for decades, centuries— forever.
I faced the sun and the moon,
I faced the moving breeze,
I faced the wind,
I faced the rain drizzle and downpour.
I faced the world and beyond.

Only now I know
I had only faced myself,
mirroring the universe
after wearing down
all my other selves—
I now face my real self.

13. Face of Allah

The thunderous storm
holds sky and earth in awesome embrace
and whispers be patient and endure,
as there is no worldly cure
in this restless suspension,
fragmented beams of light seeking
shades and colourful delight,
flickering consciousness.
Images of shadows and metaphors create things,
somethings and nothings,
all subtle deceptions
disguised as clearer perception.
Truth openly discloses
Its eternal beingness,
embracing all that is imagined,
perceived or conceived,
creations or persons
here, there or somewhere.
Movements within Divine Grace,
putting up with separation,
declaring the original and ever-present
Sacred Face.

14. Reality

It is said that
your state follows
intention and conduct,
what you believe,
desire, pursue and care for.
Yet we experience
the reality of being suspended
between sight and insight,
birth and death,
with no recall of
light before it took flight
or when you and I were not differentiated,
separated, defined or segregated.
Or when sound and sight
were not yet waves,
and reality and truth
had not descended,
and destiny was not intended.

15. Lost to Be Found

Sometimes it seems
there is only me,
challenged to see,
think and relate,
passing time through timelessness.
Then I realize that
you and others
are all like me:
denying being dumb, deaf and blind,
barely alive, lost,
comatose along the shore
of the ocean of loss,
neither sweet nor bitter,
without taste, smell or description,
belonging to the abode of preconception,
belonging to no one we know.

Yet we all assume we belong somewhere,
with names and descriptions,
but this ocean is beyond.
The light of Truth
permeates the Universe.

16. Not Fixed

Hopes and expectation
are signposts
for an orphan
with a hazy past
and uncertain future,
born premature
out of a union
rooted in separation.

A child to be taught
our confusing addictions
and other human follies,
denials, fear and loss,
challenged by our inadequacy,
futile attempts to fix our lives
or to follow the path that will
show us Presence,
the eternal perfect Now.

17. Truth and Justice

Silence is where truth resides
but justice is often vocal!
Justice lives everywhere,
local and universal;
sometimes we even hear truth.
On occasions justice is mute.
After midnight you may embrace
the silence of truth and justice,
leaving its fragrance
as landmarks along the history
of human progress,
from lights to shadows and
back again.
Where truth, justice and other perfections
were still dormant
in blissful peace and perfection.

18. Mirrors of Time

Islands of sanity
may be discovered
within the ocean of incurable madness
where shadows are justified
as messengers of light
and beams of gladness
followed thought
where they began from nothingness
seeking liberation and freedom
from illusions of creation
the Oneness camouflaged
in duplicity and deception
by flashing mirrors
within old and new memories
woven by fancy threads called time
imitating timelessness
before any past and
after all futures
yet, here and now
flickering behind the mask
of the restless guest
to be real
at all times.

19. Fields of Tulips

Fields of tulips
swaying in perfumed breeze,
free along hillsides
or in a small vase,
resting besides an old-age pensioner
with much patience—
and little pension!
Then come young visitors
to enquire and acquire
gifts and clutter,
bypassing the cemetery
where the graves declare,
"No wrong-doers are buried here!"
Good deeds this side of the hill,
evil resides the other side only.
Hearts cast in stone
untouched by the rain of love
or light of joy.
Made to acquire
more and more,
might is right!
Until the tulips return
to the silent night,
beyond the hills and past horizons
where all songs melt together
in the lake of original silence
singing in harmony and joy.

20. *Submerged*

Love's mighty power
crushed me out of me,
blasting out all illusions,
replacing them by grace
and a miracle here or there,
now or later.
A total loss of identity,
a perfect confusion.

All that is left is to pray
for deliverance,
past all observance,
beyond all plains and mountains
and other norms or sounds,
before any lips can curl or kiss
and after all words or letters
were straightened back to fluttering lives
then shrunk to floating dots,
submerged into the original, sacred plot.

21. Claiming a Name

The river ends
after numerous falls
and curvy bends—
it ends or is it lost?
At least we cease
calling it a river.
The reeds may swallow it,
or the ocean or the desert.
Some other name fills it,
such as spring, dark and unseen,
or glacier, bright and frozen.
We like names:
illusions of security
to be known.
Then another puzzle needs a name,
another human takes the blame,
another baby is born,
mother relieved for a moment,
grandmother joyful with toothless smile,
the father confused and fears sleepless nights!
But a name is already assumed
for now we know who the baby is.
A name to claim and a unique biography,
yet the same,
like all other names.

22. You Can't Look

An original article
stardust particle
winks at you
to attract and distract
tease and appease.
That which is not true
can only relate to
its cousin of falsehood,
enrobed in beauty,
claiming the throne,
asserting the light
that coloured the colourless,
traps of perfections,
dazzling magic,
segments in a play,
stuck together in time,
packaged on land,
pointing to the sky—
so where should you look?
Nowhere is safe
from distractions or destruction
or other dualities
or exploding pluralities.
Or a sacred book,
which hides behind shadows,
whenever you look.

23. Seeking Roots

Looking for roots
before sight or sound—
How old is this line?
Before the clouds,
before eternity,
when touch was the only door
to worldly connection,
how, when and where it all began,
never mind why, for now!
Hold me tight, for now,
let me feel boundaries
as I cry for freedom
from the traps of 'good behaviour'
or depression, or thoughts,
brought in by connections
from the present, past and eternity,
claiming acknowledgement,
a breeze through existence,
roots unknown,
origin unknowable,
veil of the present
smiling hypnotically,
gracefully and seductively
without a name.

24. Intimate Discovery

You wish to explore,
to learn and know
peoples, cultures and ways,
habits, forms and meanings.
Then you look for hidden horizons
beyond lands and time,
breaking barriers and boundaries,
new sights and fresh insights
where cause and effect bind and unite,
where magic and miracles are common,
where the universe is seen as a flash,
streaming along the light within the heart
where eternity resides, undisturbed,
where the quest to know
has not yet emerged,
where distance and closeness
are still submerged,
all within the core of the heart,
where the soul is the ruler
supreme and ever confirmed.

25. *Song*

With reason you try to resolve,
with heart you simply dissolve.
Mind is the toy of worldly play,
heart is the ploy of heaven's display.
The intellect differentiates,
fusion integrates,
reason discloses discernment,
soul is the light of contentment
shining from a purified heart,
enabling birds of fancy
to court, dance and sing,
seeking the abode of joy
propelled by the singing soul,
calling to itself, one and all.

26. Colours

Life is mere colour,
bright or faint,
framed or left to float,
moving clouds to highlight a sky,
a persistence with hazy substance—
true and false at the same time,
every time
a deception of no time.
Hollow and full,
me and not me,
a fallacy veiling truth,
anxiety covering blissfulness,
agitation hiding restfulness,
creation declaring eternal beingness,
lights dancing to the tune of sacredness,
by itself,
for itself,
unto itself.

The one self echoes
in countless quest-fullness,
dazzling in purposefulness,
through apparent worlds of colorfulness,
emanating and returning to the
original essence of beingness,
Oneness.

27. Reinforcing Shadows

All discussion, logic, reason—
shadow play,
palliative cover ups,
delays and distractions,
reinforced by feeble attempts
to remove falsehood.

The path is a desert
with all possibilities;
everything is lost and found
under its lights, under its shadows.
Everything agitates
and everything is at rest.

28. Allah is Greater

We are ignorant of
God's punishment and intention.
His mercy all-encompassing,
but we continue in trouble.

From this Sublime Origin
natural order flows:
to go along with the tide
is to experience an easy ride!
The pure Divine has perfected His universe,
in a sublime design.

Allah has no need or reason
for punishment or affliction.
He has already decreed that
all creation seeks His benediction
to allow divine mercy and light
to flow through us by submission.
When we transgress,
due to crucial omission,
we experience anger and separation;
yet the light of the soul
illumines every condition.

29. Natural Wilfulness

Quarrelsome sparrows
chasing, diving, rising again
in defence or offence.
Full of determination,
subtle attraction,
noisy and silent transactions
playfully fulfilling,
self-assertion,
protection, determination,
direction, destination,
attraction, repulsion
compulsion, assumption.

All of these
and other motives
perfectly governing
quarrelsome sparrows
who are only racing towards
a perfectly clear destination,

the same as
all other creations.

30. The Order of Disorder

We try to be organized,
civilized and compartmentalized;
we name every insect and germ
and dissect bees and blossoms,
resurrect dead leaders,
reincarnate heroes as airports
or renamed boulevards,
change codes and standards,
hold meetings, short and long,
local or international,
with emotions and democratic votes
arguments, suspicions and hypocrisies with notes.

Attempts to reduce anxieties and fear
all caught in our memory nests,
a life buried under the debris of hazy pasts.
Yet we strive to be more secure,
less obscure,
or fall into a disastrous holiday
when the seasonal dust storm
ravaged the beachfront
and the angry sea shattered comfort and ease,
cancelling games and noise—
days wiped out!
A biography of confused illusions,
deceptive mirrors,
reflecting denials,
pursuing mirages of lifestyles.

Dead hearts trying to organize
without knowledge or awareness
the eternal thread of divine Light
connecting in perfect order
what is known, unknown, accidents and pain.

The Eternal Presence,
ever perfect
within every heart.

31. Original Peace

Is permanent peace an illusion?
Is it attainable?
If not, then why do we yearn?

Life on earth
began with agitation
sliced from eternity,
divided then subdivided,
whilst the cosmos rotated
and surrogate Mother Earth
occupied, invaded, colonized,
providing the seeds of birth and death
in cradles of sorrow and laughter.
Anything that ever appears
will surely disappear.
Everything that is here
is on its way back there.

So how can there be permanence
in the battlefield of make-believe
where the quest of peace
is often the cause of conflict?
Whilst eternal peace,
the first and all-Pervading Peace,
is ever there, smiling
in the illumined heart.

32. The Future

What future do I have?
Or what does the future hold for me?
I wish I knew!
I wish I am assured.
I wish to be without a wish
but the future is always there!
Will it free me of fears?
Or is it the ultimate trap?
I know the future will always change
but carry the past along.
Accumulated impressions
rendered real by my faulty senses
and hazy memory
and weakened mind
and older brain
all hurtling towards a new and changed future!
The sage taught me that the world is an illusory perception
where both the past and the future are mental constructs
and the future is already here and now.
This…I have it and it has me.
Now!

33. Boredom

From the dead
come the living,
illumined stardust.
The primal stirring,
the early divine
waking up
to explore the narrow path
leading onto an endless vista,
exhilarating exhaustion,
unconditional surrender,
mindful thirst—
then mindless.
only the soul's light
consoles and radiates life
without any perception
of excitement or boredom—
only the throb of Presence.

34. Sacredness

A sacred temple:
your body,
an altar of worship,
expressing its perfection,
its universe,
with sights and insight;
here but not of here,
immense,
one essence,
finite and infinite,
perfect origin,
perfect destiny,
the One.

35. Web of Unity

All the senses,
connections,
continuations,
seen and invisible,
all are in the sacred trap
proclaiming
original connection,
eternal continuation,
Oneness.

36. Body, Mind, Heart

For children, the senses rule supreme;
the sensory is all.
With adults, it is concepts and ideas,
then sparks of spirituality.
For the awakened heart
sensuality is part of spirituality:
a natural delight of holistic integrity.
One Life-giver.

37. Gentleness

All emerged from a silent void,
utter stillness,
shadows, lights and delights.
As you approach the sanctuary
tread gently.
Silently, in awe,
then be still.
Then freeze in silence.
That is from where all emerged.
Then witness by your heart
and remember by your senses
the gentleness of the first step
announcing the whole story:
One from beginning to end.

38. Vacant Place

The house is empty now.
You feel the emptiness.
A missing heartbeat,
life incomplete.
Body, mind and heartache
quivering for the womb,
the secure home.
Oblivious to all,
seeking the lifeline,
that which is most elusive,
that which holds the universe,
that which is One!

39. To Remember You Must Forget

You are one,
or so you think!
You have one body,
you have one mind,
but to put on a new dress
you must take off the old.
To see clearly
you must move out of the fog.
To recognize truth
you have to leave your past falsehood,
ideas, memories and values.
Then there is a chance
for fresh sight,
insight,
pure light
glorious!

40. Ka'bah at Heart

Irrespective of what you do or don't,
who you will be or won't,
you will return to the same spot—
the eternal Now.
All had emerged from Oneness,
the eternally present now-ness.
To awaken to this beingness
you exercise some direction.

Born into new consciousness
out of the old cobwebs,
past experiences,
personal, cultural,
and all mental restrictions.

To experience mindlessness
and the interspace void,
where nothingness
and beingness
are seamlessly One,
time must stop.
There is singularity
before the crack of space and time
and the challenges of duality,
with you at the door of Ka'bah,
where bereftness and infinite wealth meet,
a journey completed and all prayers accepted.

41. Life's Opportunity

Every moment presents us
numerous levels of truth.
The most obvious is sensory,
then concepts and ideas,
insights and lights of delight,
connecting the eternal with the transitory,
unifying the limited with boundlessness.

The opportunity is to connect
personal life with timelessness
experienced in every aspect
before all, after all,
hidden in all,
apparent in all.

42. Just Look

Look at the sky
and wonder
Look in your heart
and vanish
Look at creation
and surrender

Be at one
with all
lost in what
the soul has always known
the One within all.

43. Dark Shadow

Once darkness
touches the heart
it can grow
casting its spell.
Only the soul's light
may dispel the darkness
cleansing shadows
letting the heart glow
in evident delight.

44. Silence

Instead of a thousand words
I enter the bliss of silence
the centre of all sounds
where melodies hide
before existence
before you and I
present within us.

This perfect silence
boundless emptiness
where the universe emanates
with its perfect smile
knowing all
and within all
ever silent
ever communicating.

45. The Party

The breeze of mercy—
an invitation to celebrate
love, light and life,
to count blessings and then
run out of numbers,
inexpressible gratitude
for Cosmic Love,
reminding earth
of its heavenly origin,
where our hearts
had not yet descended
to bless the dead earth
with eternal life—
Here our party has no beginning or end.

About the Author

Born in Karbala, Iraq, Shaykh Fadhlalla Haeri, comes from several generations of religious and spiritual leaders. After several years living and working in the west, he rediscovered the universal relevance of the Qur'an and Islamic teachings for our present day. His emphasis has been on transformative worship and refinement of conduct, as preludes to the realisation of the prevalence of Divine Grace. He considers that the purpose of life is to know and resonate with the eternal essence of the one and only Lifegiver—Allah

www.ingramcontent.com/pod-product-compliance
Lightning Source LLC
LaVergne TN
LVHW020055110826
845155LV00022B/83

* 9 7 8 1 9 1 9 8 2 6 8 1 3 *